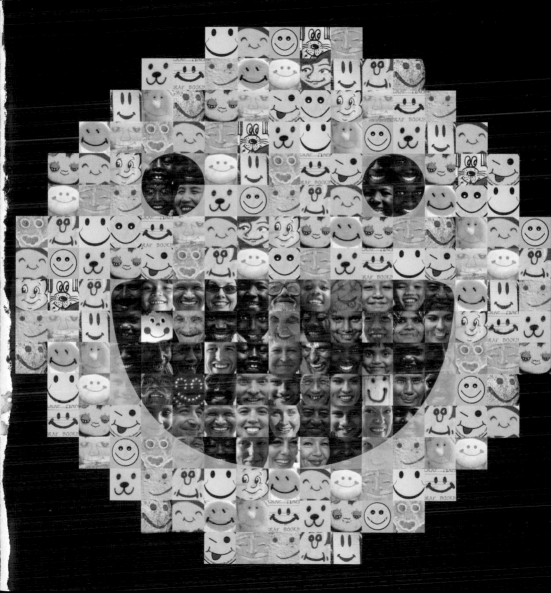

Published in 2013 by Hardie Grant Books

Hardie Grant Books (Australia)
Ground Floor, Building 1
658 Church Street
Richmond, Victoria 3121
www.hardiegrant.com.au

Hardie Grant Books (UK)
Dudley House, North Suite
34–35 Southampton Street
London WC2E 7HF
www.hardiegrant.co.uk

Cataloguing-in-Publication data is available from the National Library of Australia.

All the Happiness in the World
ISBN: 9781742706962

Concept, design and photography: Jesse Hunter
Design liaison: Mikala Robinson-Koss
Proofreading: Kate O'Donnell

www.allthehappinessintheworld.co

Colour reproduction by Splitting Image Colour Studio
Printed in China by 1010 Printing International Limited

ALL THE HAPPINESS IN THE WORLD

WHY SmILEJ fACES?

In 2010, my partner Mikala
and I embarked on a global
photographic adventure
to frame the world in our
own unique way. For
650 days, we travelled
across 44 countries,
on 6 continents, always
armed with our camera gear.

After a couple of months travelling
around our beautiful globe,
I realised there were certain 'things'
I was photographing again and again.
These 'things', which became
collections — included love hearts,
unique house numbers, intriguing
windows and taxi drivers in their
rear-view mirrors.

The collection featured here is
of smiley faces and the beaming
smiles people so openly welcomed
us with in every country we visited.
I captured hundreds of smiles in
many forms during our journey —
and a lot of these can be seen on
the cover of this book.

Happiness is
everywhere if
you just take a
moment to look.

FUN MY NIECE SILKA

KULUIN, AUSTRALIA

SOUTH MELBOURNE, AUSTRALIA

forgiveness

Berlin, GERMANY

Reykjavik, ICELAND

Be Happy

PLOVDIV, BULGARIA

Agra, INDIA

be
nice

Galata Br.
from kcrea
J.HJ & J.H.I

Istanbul, TURKEY

Copacabana, BOLIVIA

INLE LAKE, BURMA

Mae Salong, THAILAND

MELBOURNE, AUSTRALIA

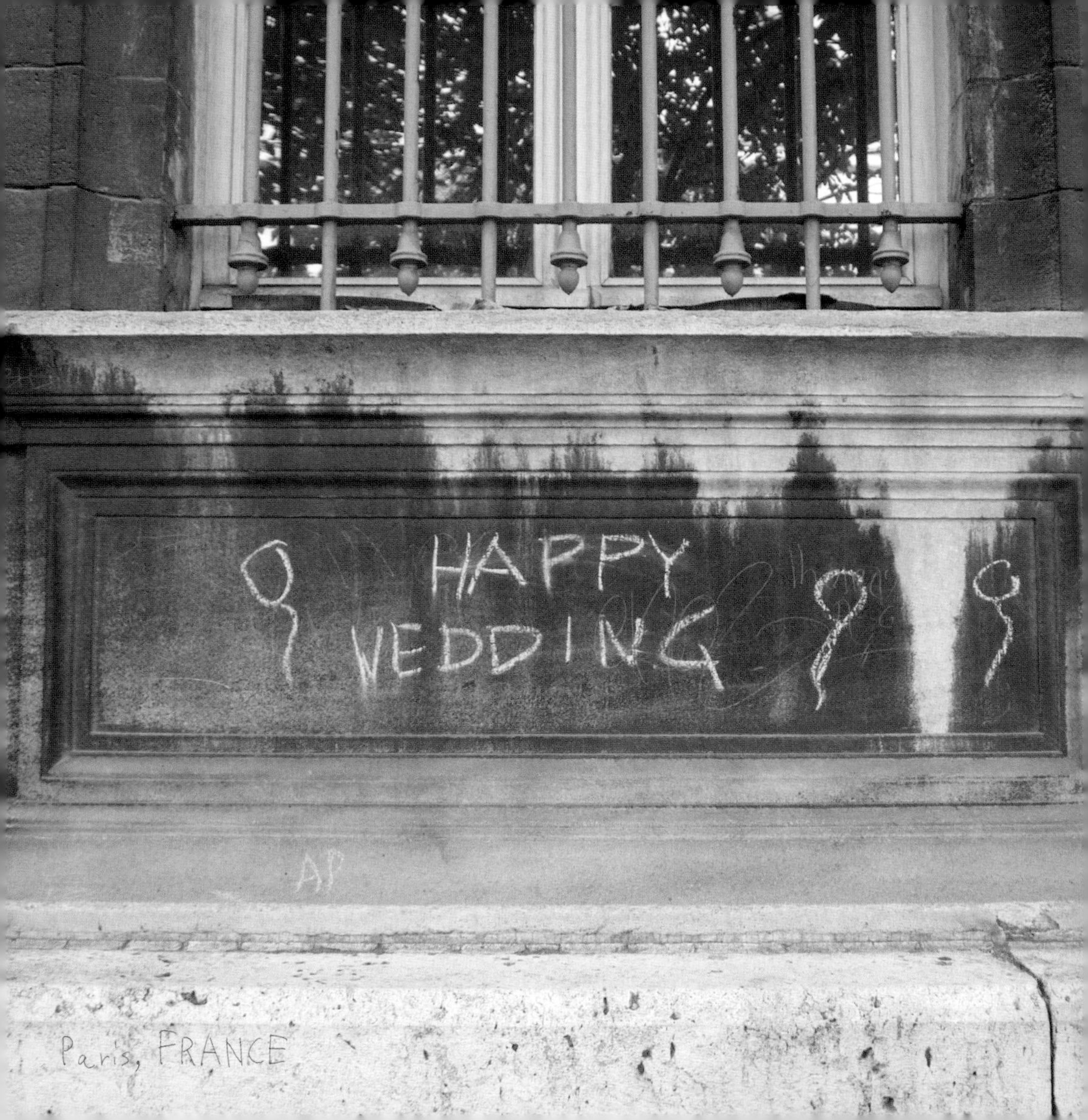

Paris, FRANCE

CAMPAGNOLA, ITALY

SMILE☺

Pamplona, SPAIN

Quito, ECUADOR

Notting Hill, ENGLAND

Notting Hill, ENGLAND

Santiago, CHILE

rome, italy

RIBADISO, SPAIN

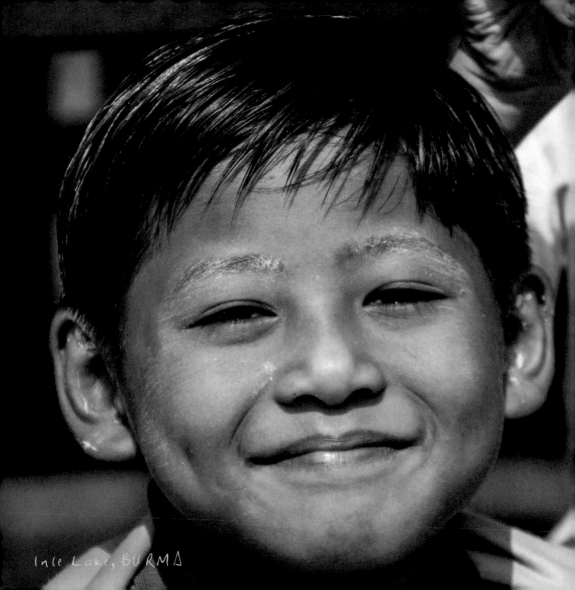
Inle Lake, BURMA

Bran, ROMANIA

Quito, ECUADOR

KAANSE (Rustenburg)

ks Suzi   Poes lek

ald & Nienie   :)

KOH TAO, THAILAND

Salar de Uyuni, BOLIVIA

Sterling Heights, USA

Kampala, UGANDA

London, ENGLAND

Rome, ITALY

NYNASHAMN, SWEDEN

28 A 🙂

NYHAVN

COPENHAGEN, DENMARK

Mandalay, BURMA

SANTA CRUZ, ECUADOR

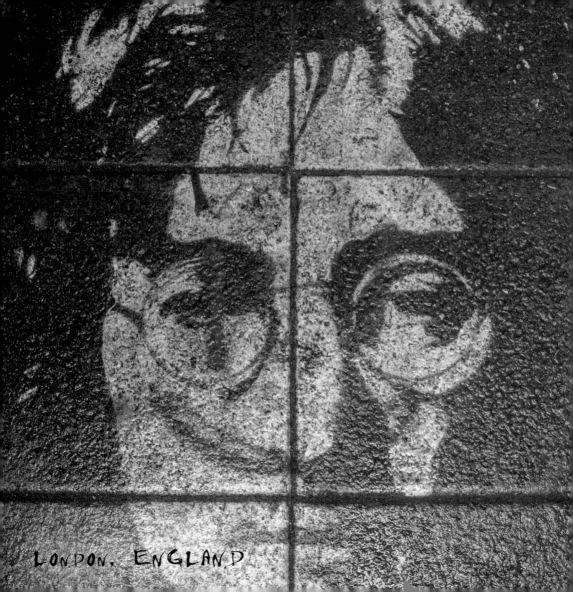

LONDON. ENGLAND

Paris. FRANCE

Varanasi, INDIA

Artiste lyrique
15 ans d'expérience professionnelle

donne
depuis 6 ans dans le 18ᵉ

COURS
DE
CHANT

Découverte patiente
de votre potentiel vocal
et musical
Approche personnalisée
Débutants bienvenus

Mᵉ Jules Joffre

Prof. Lib. inscrit à l'URSSAF

Contact : 06 86 12 17 04

jmjoffre-cours-de-chant-paris-18.fr

Ch. LAVILLAUGOUET
ASSAINISSEMENT
CANALISATIONS
01.45.35.11.11

paris. France

HELL

athens, Greece

Kampala, UGANDA

Melbourne, AUSTRALIA

Istanbul, TURKEY

Paris, FRANCE

DETROIT USA

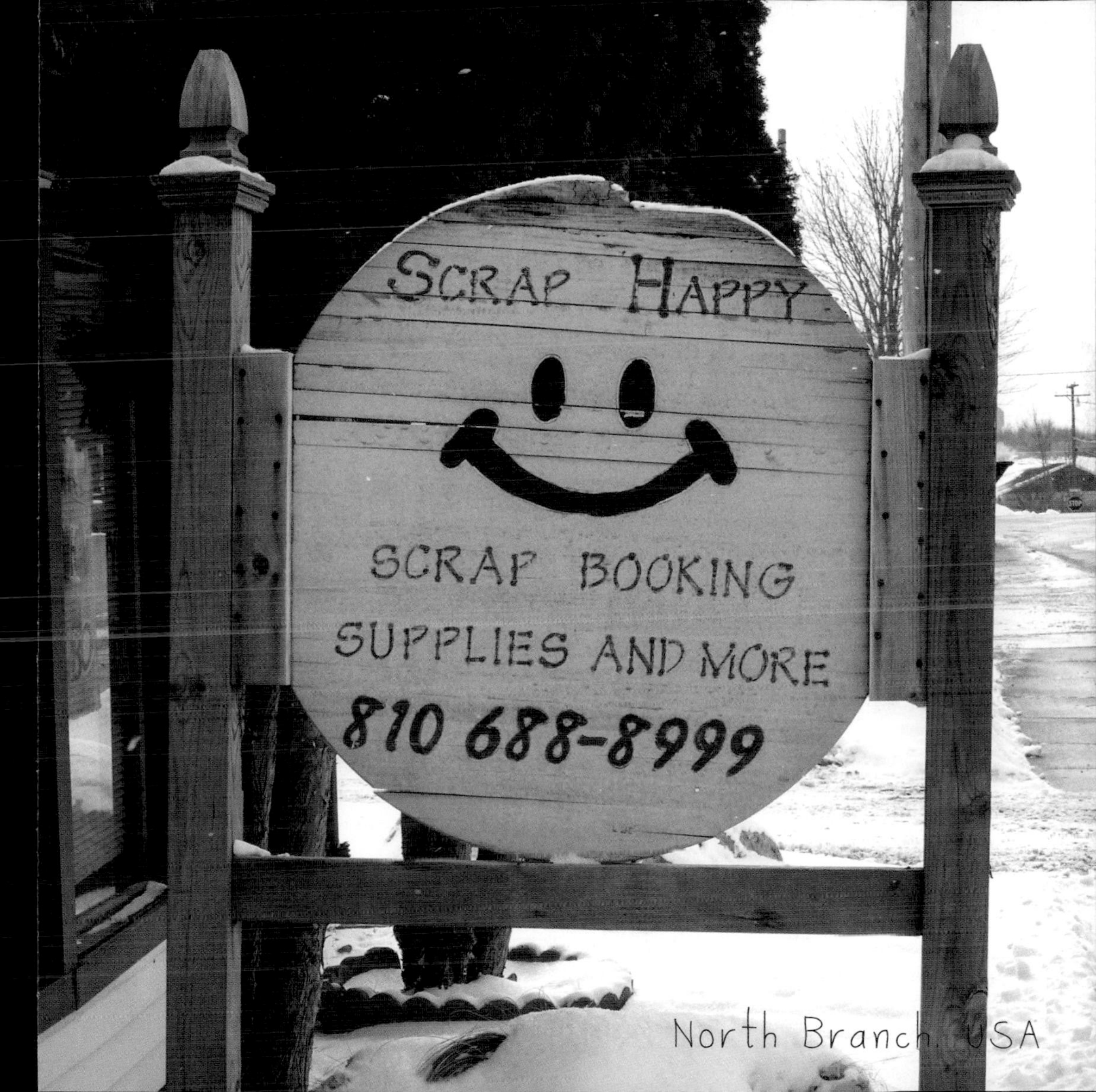

North Branch, USA

Budapest, HUNGARY

KOH TAO, THAILAND

KAMPALA UGANDA

Budapest, HUNGARY

Budapest HUNGARY

Plovdiv, BULGARIA

Galapagos Islands, ECUADOR

Toronto, CANADA

BARCELONA, SPAIN

HAVE 2 PAINT,
LOOKING 4 RIDE...
ANYWHERE!!!

BERLIN, GERMANY

PAMPLONA, SPAIN

Kampala, UGANDA

Rabat, MOROCCO

ROME, ITALY

Yangon, BURMA

CURRY 7

Berlin, GERMANY

TRENCIN, SLOVAKIA

Morgade: SPAIN

Melbourne, AUSTRALIA

Pamplona, SPAIN

Pushkar, INDIA

Mob N.
9887166910

वेटर श्री नाग सिंह राजत

राधा कौर राजनूर

Essaouira, MOROCCO

Happy
Multi Use Soap

Nyaung Shwe, BURMA

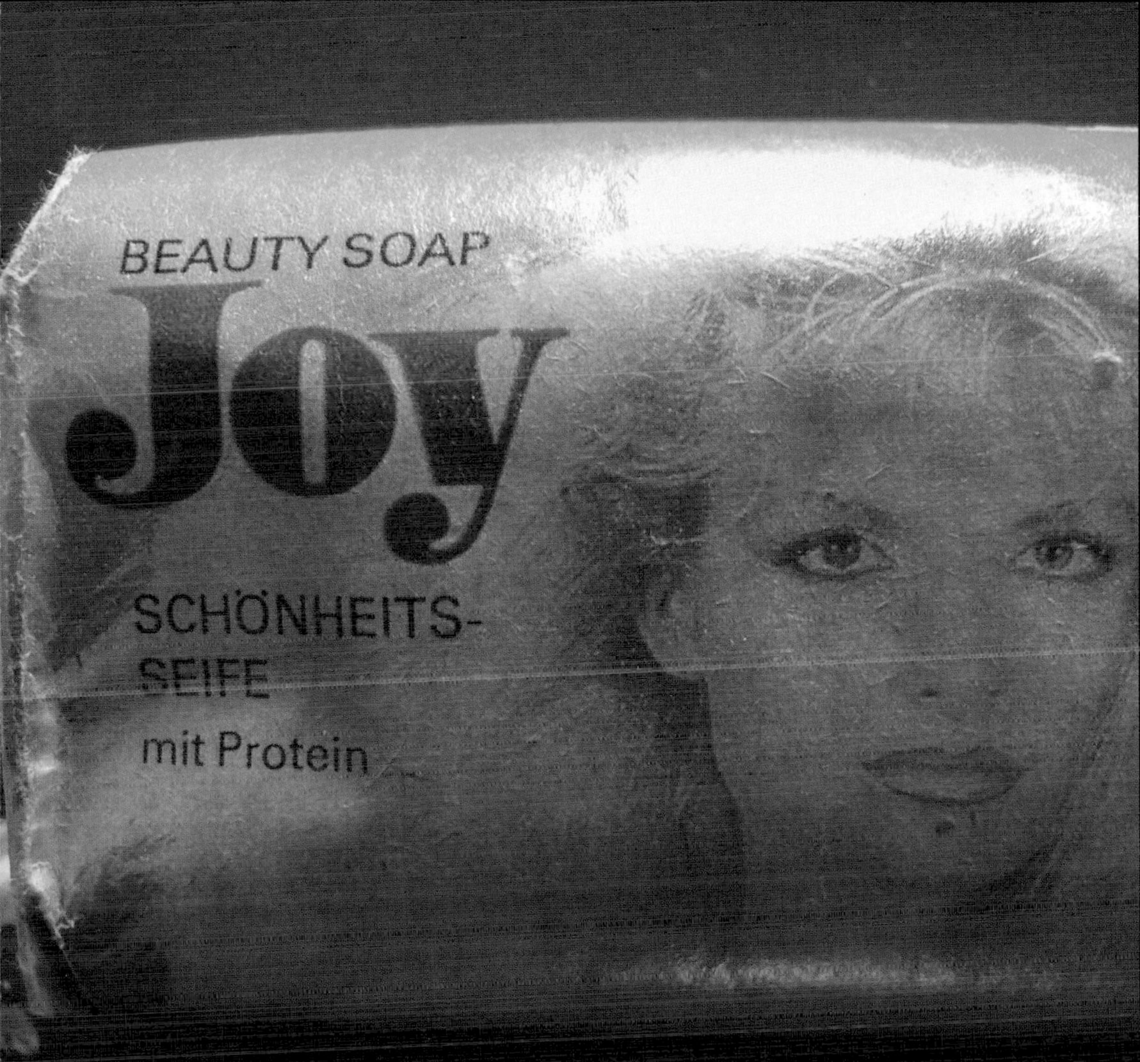
BEAUTY SOAP
Joy
SCHÖNHEITS-
SEIFE
mit Protein

COPENHAGEN, DENMARK

Kampala, UGANDA

Valparaiso, CHILE

Santiago, CHILE

Amsterdam, THE NETHERLANDS

Santiago, CHILE

Valle de la Mina, PANAMA

聚寶盆

ขอม

ศรีสาย

ยินดีต้อนรับ

สวัสดี

SUVARNABHUMI, THAILAND

Amazon Jungle, PERU

Amazon Jungle, PERU

Llubljiana, SLOVENIA

Galapagos Islands, ECUADOR

North Branch, USA

GAYLORD, USA

BERLIN, GERMANY

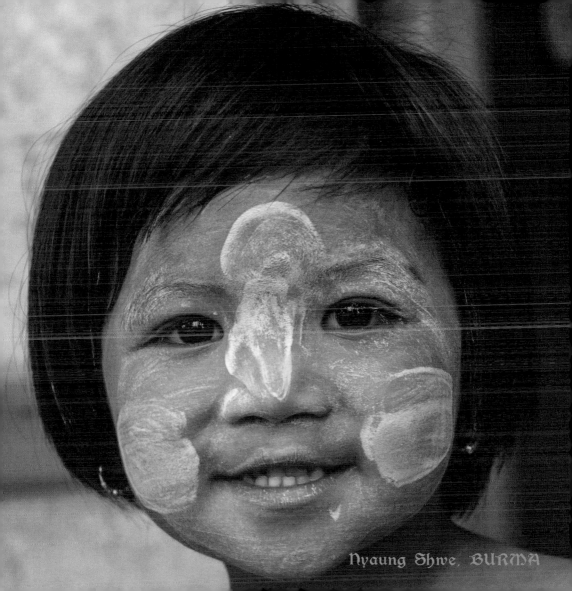

Nyaung Shwe, BURMA

Prague, CZECH REPUBLIC

Atlanta, USA

CITY RD

BOURNE UNI

E COFFEE ALL DAY

06 MARCH 2013

-BOYD / 207 CITY RD

-MELBOUENE UNI

FREE COFFEE ALL DAY

JOIN US

South Melbourne, AUSTRALIA

MANDALAY, BURMA

BE FREE
SER LIBRE

Valle de la Mina, PANAMA

Bagan, BURMA

Maroochydore, AUSTRALIA

SALAR DE UYUNI, BOLIVIA

Dubai, UAE

Suggestion

WEB PHONE

Suvarnabhumi, THAILAND

Siem Reap. CAMBODIA

MEGADETH

THE PLACE TO BE

I LOVE TRUE THAT

Positive future

THANKS YOU FOR

MARNIE
ED
FAH

FREE Let

PIZZA HUH?
YES, PIZZA

ANGKOR

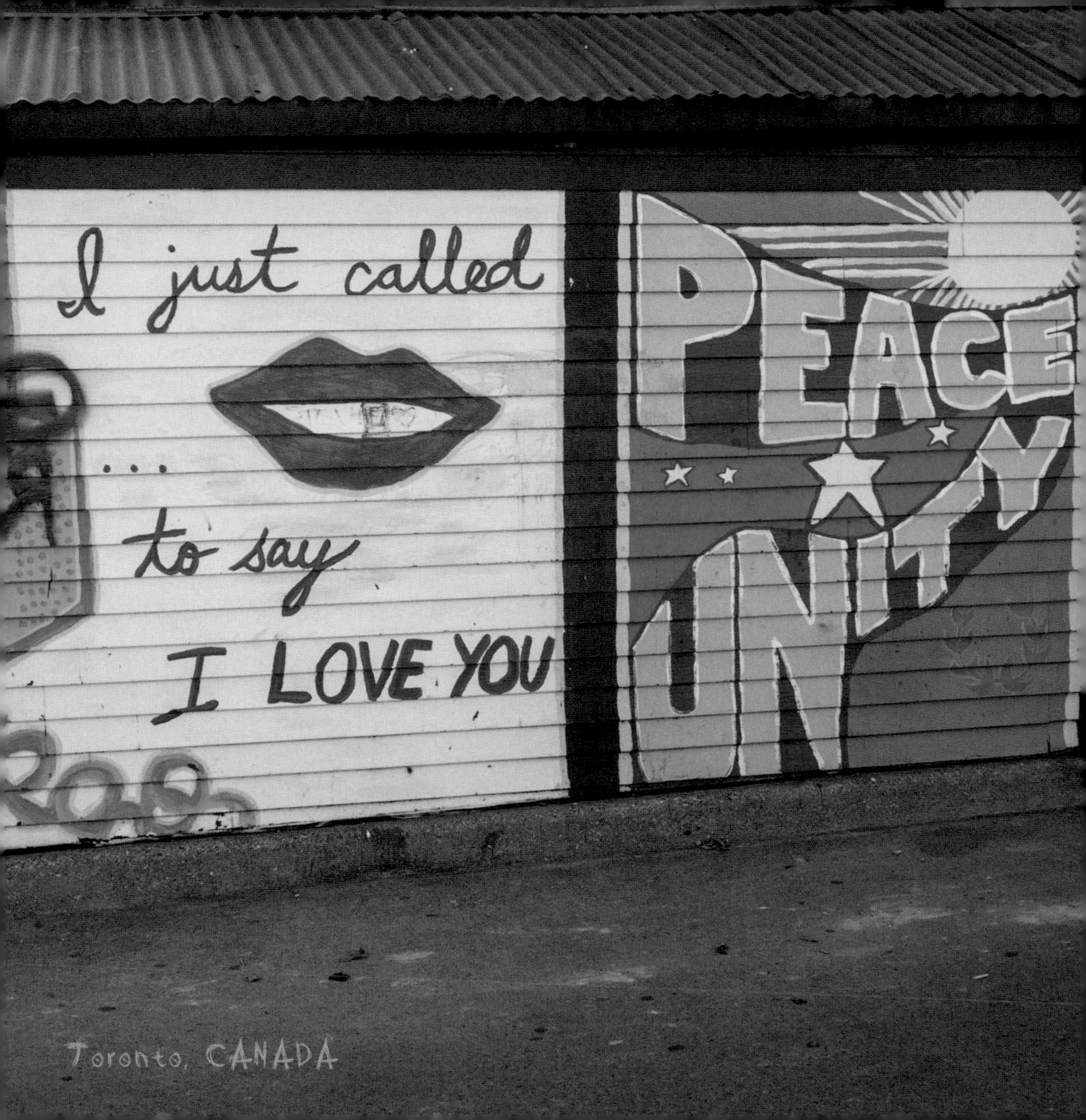

Toronto, CANADA

notting hill, england

Aarau, SWITZERLAND

Gotland, SWEDEN

TORONTO, CANADA

BRAN, ROMANIA

Jaipur, INDIA

Guamote, ECUADOR

Santiago, CHILE

london, england

KAMPALA, UGANDA

Ciao
Tina
Linda

FLoRence. itALy

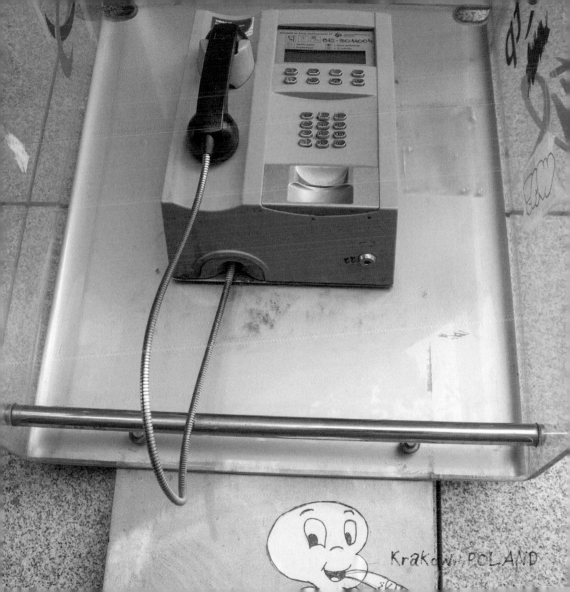

Kraków, POLAND

Petra, JORDAN

Happy

Happy You

Happy Me

Happy You

Happy You

kcal 110 6%

Copenhagen, DENMARK

Varanasi, INDIA

Zaanse Schons, THE NETHERLANDS

Amsterdam, THE NETHERLANDS

ရှိုင်မုံး

ချစ်သော မီ မင်းရဲ့ဘဝပျော်ရွှင်ပါစေ

MANDALAY, BURMA

Colchani, BOLIVIA

Kuluin, AUSTRALIA

El agua es vida

UYUNI, BOLIVIA

San Francisco, USA

Trencin, SLOVAKIA

Copenhagen, DENMARK

SALE
150

DELHI, INDIA

150
NO TRY

150
NO TRY
B

Koh Tao, THAILAND

Makuyuni, TANZANIA.

Khajuraho, INDIA

Veliko Tarnovo, BULGARIA

Chiang Rai, THAILAND

nickec
N

PTT

AMSTERDAM, THE NETHERLANDS

Jaisalmer, INDIA

NO DEJES
A DE
SONREIR !
26-11
2004

Pamplona, SPAIN

I want to thank you from the bottom of my happy heart for joining me on this journey to discover

ALL THE HAPPINESS IN THE WORLD

entebbe. uganda

Mikala, your beaming
smile lights my life.
Danke schön, gracias,
and thank you always.

Abundant happiness
and thanks to my
family and friends
for your constant
love, support and
encouragement of my
creative endeavours.

Danke schön to
everyone who
housed or fed
Mikala and I during
our journey around
the world.

Gracias to all who
have shared their
smiles and happiness
with me during my
time on this beautiful
planet we live on.

Chiguana Desert, BOLIVIA

Where there is Happiness, there is Peace.

- Jesse Hunter

www.allthehappinessintheworld.co